HoME is where we live

Life at a Shelter through a Young Girl's Eyes

Photographs by
B. L. Groth

Book Design by
Kimiko

CORNERSTONE PRESS CHICAGO
CHICAGO, ILLINOIS

To the children and women who have lived
at Cornerstone Community Outreach Center.

Published by Cornerstone Press Chicago, the publishing arm of Jesus People USA Covenant Church. Jesus People USA is a community of Christians serving the poor, the homeless, and the elderly in the Uptown neighborhood of Chicago.On a national and international level, Jesus People is known for Cornerstone *magazine, Grrr recordS (Resurrection Band, Cauzin' efekt, CRASHDOG, the Crossing, Grace and Glory, and Glenn Kaiser), and Cornerstone Festival. If you would like more information about Jesus People USA and its outreaches, write Cornerstone Press Chicago at 939 W. Wilson Ave., Chicago, IL 60640.*

ISBN 0-940895-34-X

Printed in Hong Kong
98 97 96 95 4 3 2 1

Library of Congress Cataloging-in-Publication Data

Kimiko, 1971–
    Home is where we live: life in a shelter through a young girl's eyes / illustrated by Kimiko; photographs by B. L. Groth; edited by Jane Hertenstein.
       p. cm.
    Summary: Photographs with brief text chronicle a seven-month stay at a homeless shelter where a ten-year-old girl felt scared at first but later felt safe.
    ISBN 0-940895-34-X
    1. Homeless children—United States—Juvenile literature.   2. Shelters for the homeless—United States—Juvenile literature.
[1. Homeless persons. 2. Shelters for the homeless.]   I. Groth, Bonnie Lee, 1965–
ill. II. Hertenstein, Jane, 1958–   .   III. Title.
HV4505.K55 1995
362.7'08'6942—dc20
                                                 95-34297
                                               CIP
                                               AC

We moved to the shelter this year—Mamma, me, William,
and our baby sister, LaTasha.

I was scared at first.
All the kids and mothers live in one room. William cried that night.
I cried too, but I didn't let anybody hear me.

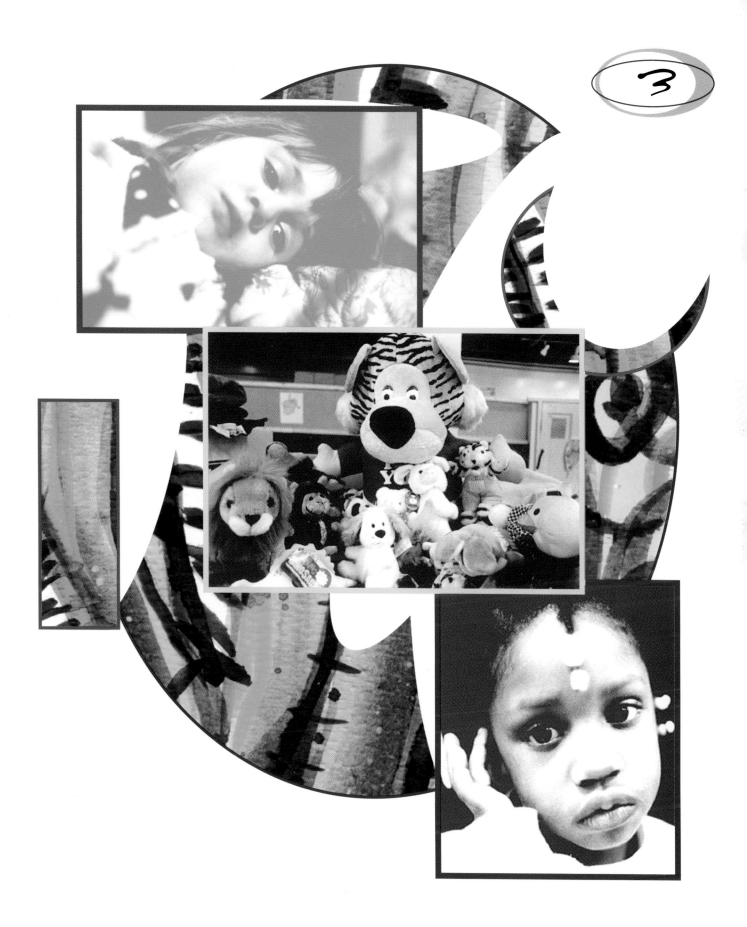

Mamma put up her pictures, and I have my special pillow.
We try to make it a home.

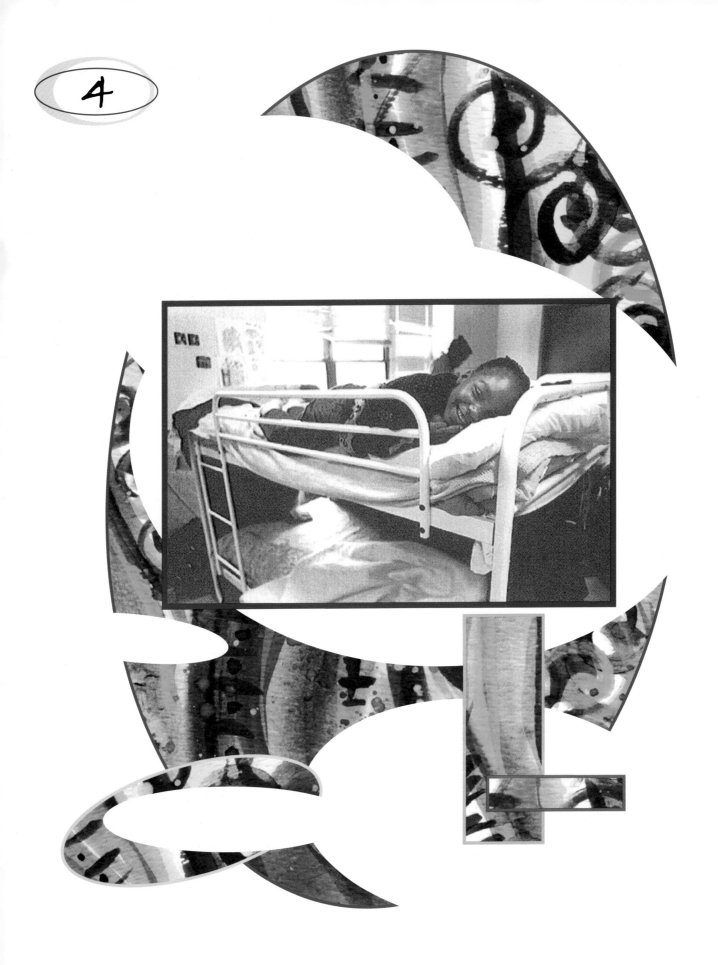

Mamma gave me the top bunk.

I hear the "L" train roar by my window.

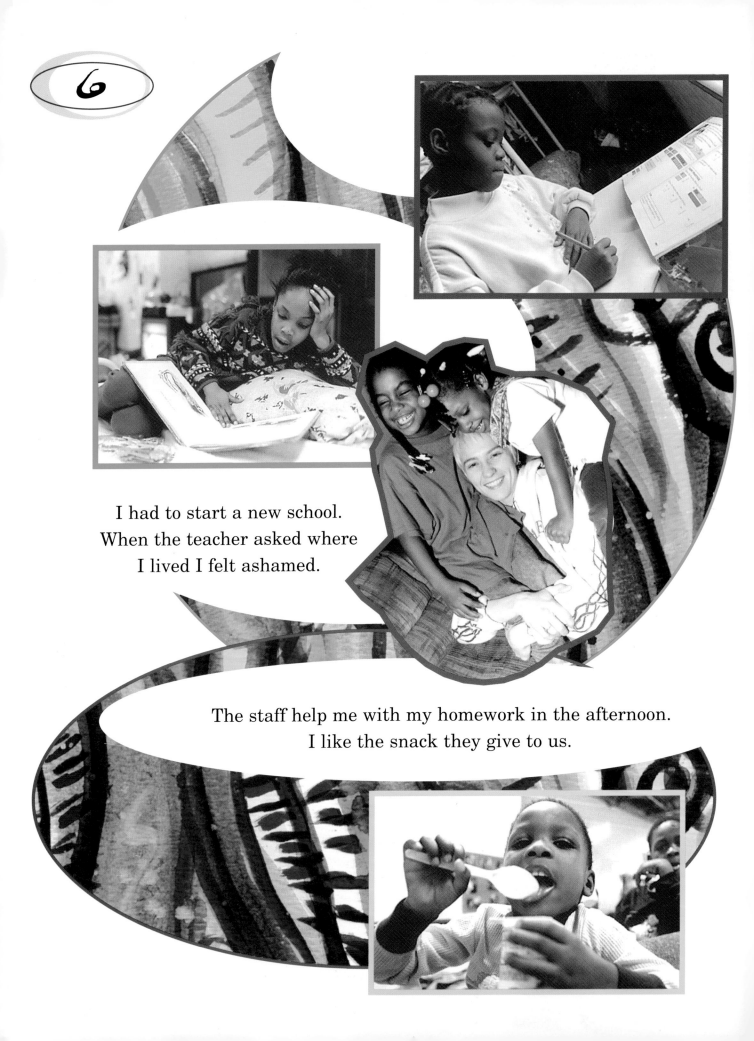

I had to start a new school.
When the teacher asked where
I lived I felt ashamed.

The staff help me with my homework in the afternoon.
I like the snack they give to us.

William plays in the daycare. He has learned
some new songs and can say his ABCs.
One day I helped William color his picture.

They put our artwork on the walls.

We do a lot of fun stuff. We have birthday parties all the time.

With so many people living together someone
is always having a birthday.

Christmas at the shelter is special. All the little
kids got to be in a play.

My brother was a shepherd. I wanted to be Mary,
but at least I got to be an angel.

On Christmas day we all got lots and lots of presents.

My little brother got a cool truck. I got
a baby doll that spins around.

In the wintertime darkness comes early.
I really like Girl Scouts and girls' group in the evening.

Girls' group is fun. We all get together with Angel and the other
staff to make cookies or maybe go to a restaurant. One time
we went ice-skating downtown. I had never ice-skated before.

Sometimes I get mad at all the little kids getting into my stuff.

I wish I could have a room of my own.

Mamma talks on the telephone hoping to get an apartment.
She goes to classes. I see her sad and at other times
laughing with the other moms.

If Mamma is busy with the baby, someone else helps me get dinner.
It is like a great big family.

The weather is getting warmer.
We go to parks and stuff after school and on weekends.

Crystal's daddy comes to visit. I wish my daddy would come by.
I still don't understand why we can't all live together anymore.

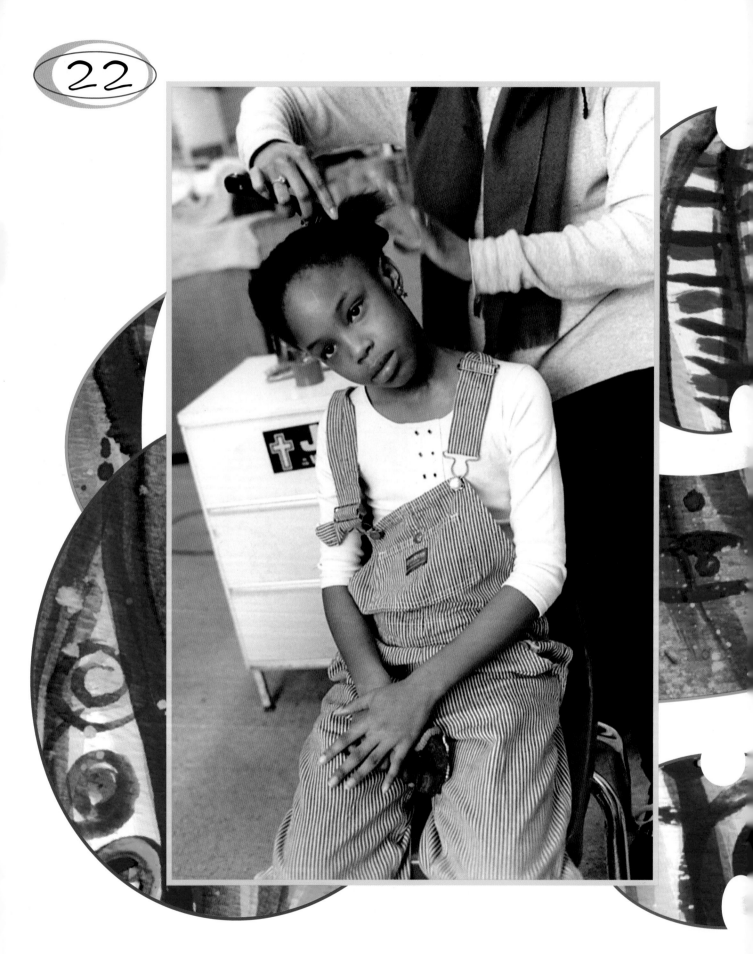

I'm getting more and more used to the shelter.

I don't like the lines at the sinks in the morning. I also miss my mom's cooking.

Today all the kids decorated eggs for Easter.
Sunday we're going to dress up for church and have an egg hunt.

I hope I find the prize egg.

Mamma found an apartment.
We're going to get our stuff out of storage and move real soon.

We packed up all our clothes and bedding. I'm going to give away some of my toys. Mamma said we've collected a whole new houseful of stuff while living at the shelter.

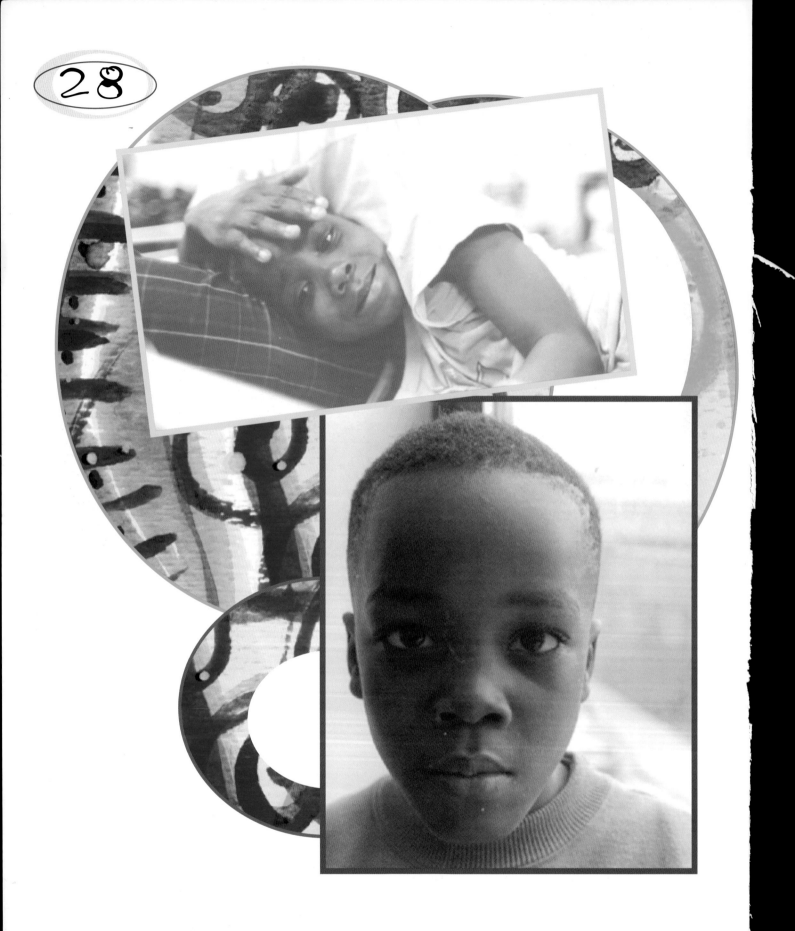

Last night I heard the new boy in the bunk next to me crying.
I think he is scared like I used to be.

I dream about our new home.

THE END

I'm going to miss my friends.
The shelter was a good place to stay. I felt safe.